Five-Minute FRIENDSHIP STARTERS

A Sesame Street Guide to Making a Friend

Marie-Therese Miller

Lerner Publications ◆ Minneapolis

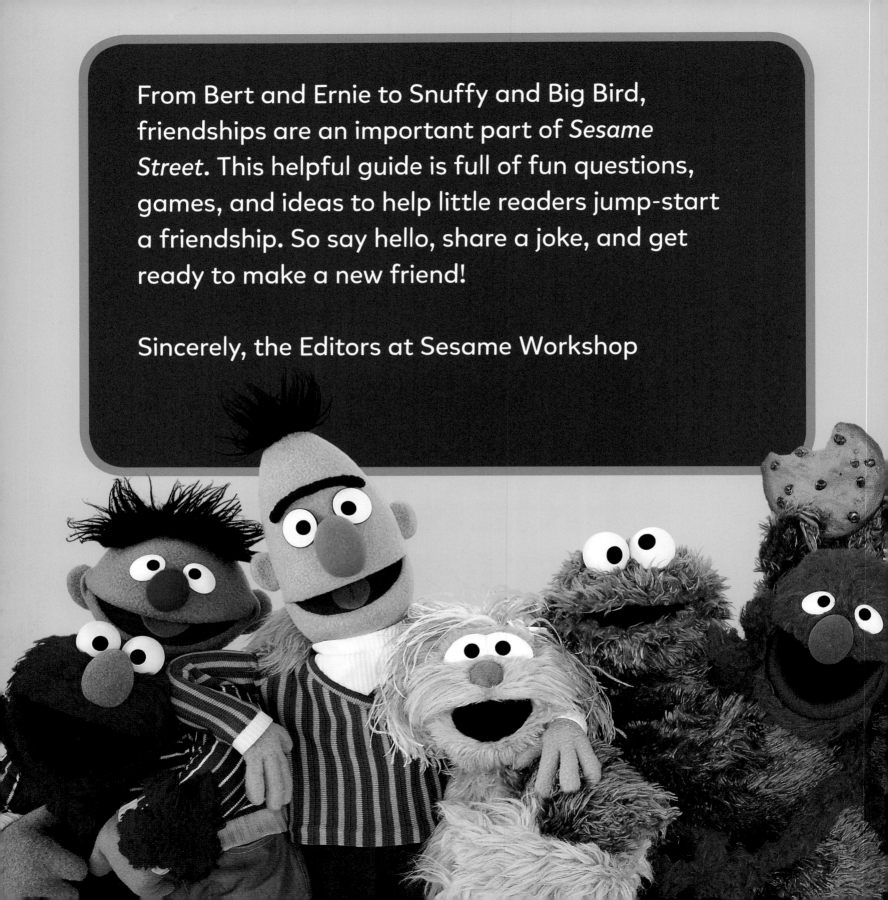

From Bert and Ernie to Snuffy and Big Bird, friendships are an important part of *Sesame Street*. This helpful guide is full of fun questions, games, and ideas to help little readers jump-start a friendship. So say hello, share a joke, and get ready to make a new friend!

Sincerely, the Editors at Sesame Workshop

TABLE OF CONTENTS

FRIENDS ARE FUN!

Friends are special.

I enjoy spending time with my ol' buddy Bert.

It's fun to play and pretend together.

There are lots of ways to make new friends. Let's find out how!

MAKE NEW FRIENDS

To meet a new friend, smile and say, "Hi!"
Tell them your name and ask their name.

Ask questions to learn more about your new friend. Try asking if they have brothers or sisters or any pets. Be sure to tell your friend about yourself too.

I have a cousin named Tamir! Do you have any cousins?

Questions to Try!

What games do you
like to play?

What do you want to be
when you grow up?

What's your favorite color?

If you were an animal, what
animal would you be?

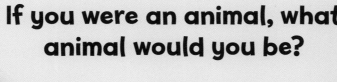

9

Talk about your favorite things. Find out your friend's favorite food, sport, or book. Then tell them yours!

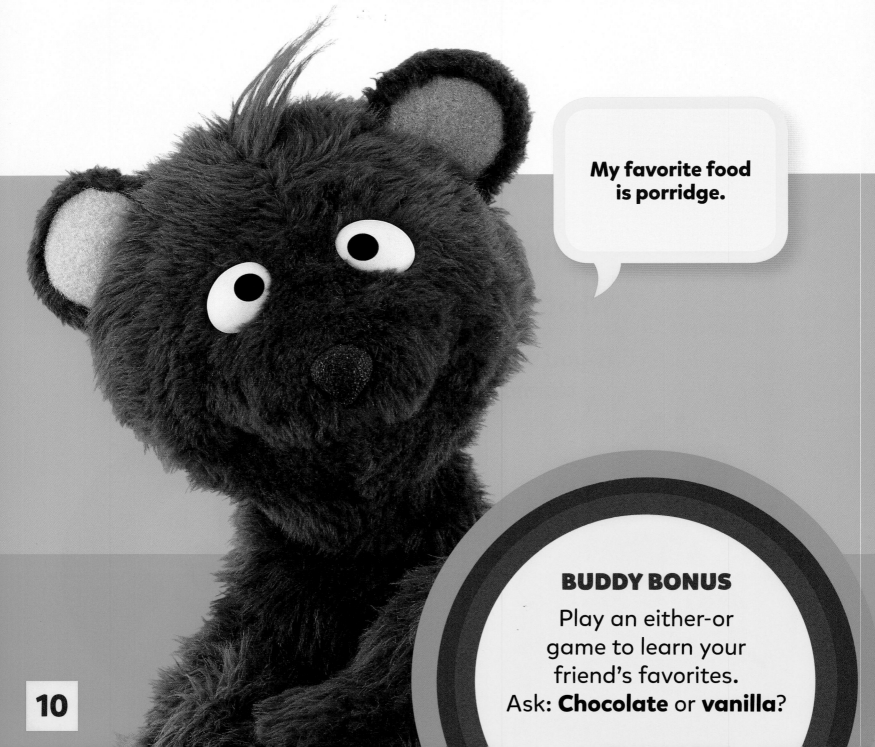

My favorite food is porridge.

BUDDY BONUS

Play an either-or game to learn your friend's favorites.
Ask: **Chocolate** or **vanilla**?

Questions to Try!

Which do you like best?

Singing or dancing?

Bananas or apples?

Dogs or cats?

Soccer or basketball?

Friends play together.

Go on a treasure hunt! One person hides toys around the room. The other looks for them. Take turns hiding and finding the toys.

I play trash hunt with Slimey.

Pretending is fun with a friend. Imagine you are explorers.

I like to pretend the jungle gym is a real jungle!

The playground swings are your airplanes.
The slide is a mountain to climb.

Friends laugh together. Make the funniest faces you can. Whoever makes the other laugh first wins!

16

BUDDY BONUS

Learn a new joke and tell it to your friend!

What do you get when you cross a fish with an elephant? Swimming trunks!

Snuffy can always make me laugh!

17

Practice tongue twisters together. "Rubber baby buggy bumpers" and "A big black bug bit a big black bear" are two tricky ones!

If you can't be together in person, try an online show-and-tell. Share a special item or a story from your life, and listen when it's your friend's turn to share.

21

Try this listening game. One player is Elmo. They say, "Elmo says" and give the other player an action to do. If Elmo doesn't say, "Elmo says," don't move. Take turns being Elmo.

Think of things you like about your friend and tell them.

I tell Julia her drawings are magical!

BUDDY BONUS

Make a card for your friend to show you appreciate them.

Kind Words to Try!

You always share your toys.

I love the pictures that you draw.

You're a really fast runner!

Wow! You tell really funny jokes.

Friends can teach each other new things. Have your friend teach you their favorite sport or game.

Friends share. You and your friend could share toys. Then you would both have fun!

29

You can find friends anywhere.

Look around in your neighborhood, at school, or at the playground. It doesn't take long to make a new friend!

GLOSSARY

appreciate: to value somebody or something

favorite: something that a person likes best

imagine: to form an idea or picture in your mind

pretend: to make believe

tongue twister: a series of words that is hard to say correctly

LEARN MORE

Hunter, Charlotte. *What Friends Do*. North Mankato, MN: Rourke, 2019.

Pettiford, Rebecca. *Different Interests*. Minneapolis: Bullfrog Books, 2018.

Rotner, Shelley, and Sheila M. Kelly. *All Kinds of Friends*. Minneapolis: Millbrook Press, 2018.

INDEX

PHOTO ACKNOWLEDGMENTS

Photos by: Monkey Business Images/Shutterstock.com, p. 5 (top); FatCamera/Getty Images, pp. 5 (right), 12 (lower); JGI/Jamie Grill/Getty Images, pp. 5 (lower), 16 (right); SDI Productions/Getty Images, p. 6; wundervisuals/Getty Images, p. 12 (top); JohnnyGreig/Getty Images, p. 12 (right); Krakenimages.com/Shutterstock.com, p. 16 (top); baona/Getty Images, p. 16 lower; MarsBars/Getty Images, p. 18; Inti St Clair/Getty Images, p. 20; Tatiana Popova/Shutterstock.com, p. 21 (third from top); Iakov Filimonov/Shutterstock.com, p. 23; Golden Pixels LLC/Shutterstock.com, p. 26; lisegagne/Getty Images, p. 28; Patrick Foto/Shutterstock.com, p. 30 (top); ktaylorg/Getty Images, p. 30 (lower).

To all of my cherished friends, especially my best friend, Donna, and my cousin-friends, Kathleen, Aileen, and Sue Ann

Lerner Publications Company
An imprint of Lerner Publishing Group, Inc.
241 First Avenue North
Minneapolis, MN 55401 USA

For reading levels and more information, look up this title at www.lernerbooks.com.

Main body text set in Mikado. Typeface provided by HVD.

Editor: Alison Lorenz **Designer:** Laura Otto Rinne
Photo Editor: Cynthia Zemlicka
Lerner team: Katy Prozinski

Library of Congress Cataloging-in-Publication Data

Names: Miller, Marie-Therese, author.
Title: Five-minute friendship starters : a Sesame Street guide to making a friend / Marie-Therese Miller.
Description: Minneapolis : Lerner Publications, [2022] | Includes bibliographical references and index. | Audience: Ages 4–8 | Audience: Grades K–1 | Summary: "Making a new friend is easy with help from Sesame Street! Young readers learn fun ways to approach, get to know, and have fun with a new friend—in just five minutes!"– Provided by publisher.
Identifiers: LCCN 2021007527 (print) | LCCN 2021007528 (ebook) | ISBN 9781728439174 (library binding) | ISBN 9781728444888 (ebook)
Subjects: LCSH: Friendship in children–Juvenile literature.
Classification: LCC HQ784.F7 M55 2022 (print) | LCC HQ784.F7 (ebook) | DDC 302.34083–dc23

LC record available at https://lccn.loc.gov/2021007527
LC ebook record available at https://lccn.loc.gov/2021007528

Manufactured in the United States of America
1-49824-49691-7/13/2021